PERSONA

A Proven Step-By-Step Guide to Identifying and Attracting Profitable Customers to Your New Business

I0489167

GATHONI NJENGA

FRANK DAPPAH

ISBN:9781099351150

DEDICATION

This book is dedicated to "the little guy." The Freelancers, Mompreneurs, the seasoned small business owner, and the ones just getting started.

To anyone who has taken or thinking about taking the first step towards entrepreneurship. This one's for you!

Would you like me to give you a formula for success? It's quite simple, really: Double your rate of failure. You are thinking of failure as the enemy of success. But it isn't at all. You can be discouraged by failure or you can learn from it, so go ahead and make mistakes. Make all you can. Because remember that's where you will find success.

-Thomas J. Watson

CONTENTS

INTRODUCTION

We believe the American dream is still alive and well. Never has there been an era with greater potential for self-starters like yourself to rise and strive for self-determination.

The U.S. economy is as strong as it's ever been. Unemployment is at an all-time low and The Stock Market is at an all-time high.

Moreover, the proliferation of the internet and all things tech present entrepreneurial-minded folks of all backgrounds with enormous opportunity to build long-lasting wealth. True Wealth.

No! You are not crazy

So, you just started a new business venture, and you have many questions. Just like millions of folks around the globe, it looks like you have decided to go the entrepreneurial route rather than a J.O.B. or perhaps starting a new business is simply a second or third act for you.

I am sure there have been times when you have wondered to yourself, "Am I making a mistake?" "I mean, who starts a business at my age?" Well, many people do. According to Entrepreneur Magazine, over half a million folks just like you decide to become Entrepreneurs every month, and out of that number, over 24 percent of these new business owners are over the age of 55, up from 14 percent just a few years ago.

About a quarter of all new business's owners are seniors,

retired, or just trying their hands at something new. So, you see, you are not crazy, and you are not alone. Keep your eye on the prize, stay focused on growing a profitable business, and you will do just fine.

We wrote this book to provide folks like you with a practical straight-to-the-point, no B.S. guide to building and growing a robust, bottom-line-oriented business. In this book, we try to accomplish this by focusing specifically on the areas of establishing a distinct brand identity and attracting profitable customers. We chose to narrowly focus on these particular areas because we believe these fundamental dynamics are essential to the success of any business.

If you are like us, then you love numbers. Nothing, to us, drives home an argument better than some numbers, data, stats, whatever you want to call it. In this book, we will, from time to time, break out some numbers to help drive home

some point or argument we are trying to make. We hope you

don't mind.

Why are you really doing this?

We don't need to tell you that in today's world, "being in business" means different things to different people. For some, profitability takes a backseat to a sense of accomplishment and emotional fulfillment. For others, ourselves included, business is just that: Business and our #1 focus is Money, Greenbacks, Moolah, Cheese, Chedda, Guap. You get my point.

Whatever your reasons for going into business may be, we strongly recommend that you take some time, pour yourself a glass of Absolute 100, or whatever your drink of choice is, and have a super honest, heart-to-heart conversation with yourself. Carefully consider the actual reason(s) you have decided to take this long and inevitably challenging journey.

Why are you really doing this? Consider the potential adverse impact this route comes with, which will compound if a general lack of focus exists or persists on your part.

Being honest with yourself about your real reasons for going into business for yourself will go a long way to help you create a streamlined operation with checks, balances, systems, and processes, all working together towards your ultimate goal. Again, whatever that may be.

Small Businesses are powerful

There is nothing "Small" about Small business. No, ma'am! As a Small Business Owner, you are part of an elite, powerful, ubiquitous component of the American economy. The economic future of the world rests in your hands. Small business means power.

Think I am messing with you? Well, consider these stats:

International Trade

On average, a total of about 300k companies export goods per year. Ninety-seven percent of those companies are Small Companies, Small firms (firms with less than 500 employees), generate about 32 percent of the United States' $1.3 trillion in total exports. Up from 28 percent in less than 15 years. (Source: I.T.A.)

Year	Number of U.S. Goods Exporters					Value of U.S. Exports of Goods ($million)				
	Total	Small Business		Large Business		Total	Small Business		Large Business	
		Number	%	Number	%		Value	%	Value	%
2006	245,945	239,287	97.3	6,658	2.7	$910,465	$262,999	28.9	$647,466	71.1
2007	268,526	261,424	97.4	7,102	2.6	$1,034,046	$314,142	30.4	$719,904	69.6
2008	289,711	282,603	97.5	7,108	2.5	$1,150,903	$361,967	31.5	$788,936	68.5
2009	276,643	270,053	97.6	6,590	2.4	$940,410	$308,927	32.9	$631,483	67.1
2010	293,988	287,498	97.8	6,490	2.2	$1,140,406	$384,940	33.8	$755,466	66.2
2011	303,509	296,817	97.8	6,692	2.2	$1,325,046	$443,598	33.5	$881,448	66.5
2012	305,669	298,782	97.7	6,887	2.3	$1,381,728	$450,618	32.6	$931,110	67.4
2013	304,223	297,343	97.7	6,880	2.3	$1,400,955	$471,069	33.6	$929,886	66.4

Source: U.S. Census Bureau, A Profile of U.S. Importing and Exporting Companies

Employment

You cannot ignore the impact that small companies have on

the overall job market. Many Americans, about 58.9 million or 47 percent to be precise, work, directly or indirectly for a Small Business.

A more significant percentage of this overall figure comes from Organizations with fewer than 100 employees. With the current Unemployment rate hovering around 4.1 percent, an all-time low, it is safe to say that Small Business is booming.

Figure 1: United States Employment by Business Size (Employees)

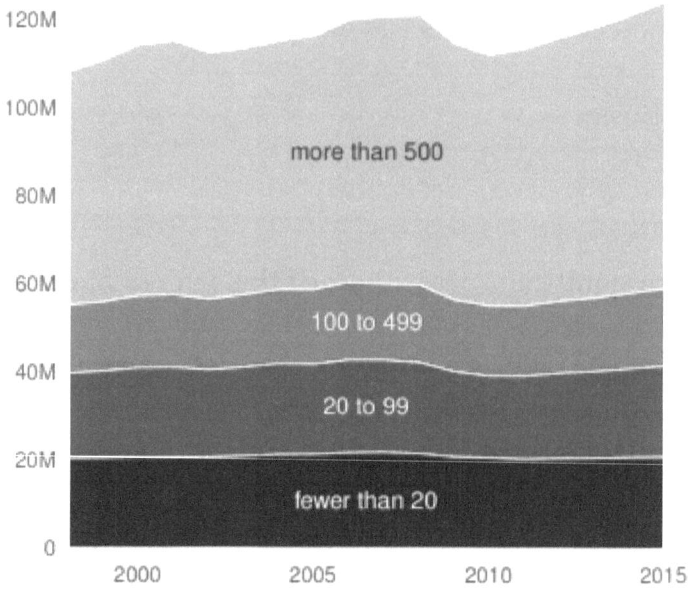

"People will buy what they need or want, not what you need them to

want or want them to need."

Frank Dappah

CHAPTER 1

PLANNING FOR SUCCESS

What do you do again?

Since you are probably at the initial stages of building your business, we do not expect you to have a complete and concise answer to this question just yet. The truth is, over the next five to ten years, your product or service offerings will undergo various cosmetic or fundamental changes. Most of these changes will be in response to shifting social and economic conditions in the marketplace.

Other changes will occur as a result of you trying to expand your business or take advantage of a growing market trend. You are probably old enough to remember a time when America Online (AOL) sold dial-up internet access via mail. A time when you would have had to physically go into a video rental store to rent a movie (On DVD or tape) for the weekend. Times have changed, and companies in these markets have had to adapt to changes caused by technology and consumers' needs and wants.

As you proceed to flesh out your brand identity and business model, try to answer the question of "What do you do again?" in the simplest terms possible. Try to answer this question in a way that would require no follow up questions to clarify. A statement of what you do should also convey parts of your value proposition. So, for example, Walmart is not just a Grocer, but a low-cost one.

What is the Purpose of your Business?

At any point in the evolution of your business, it is essential to maintain a clear-eyed sense of purpose. This purpose may, at times, serve as the inspiration for your mission and vision statements. You will want to be very clear to yourself about why you are in business, where you hope to take your business, and what you want to get out of it.

Having this streamlined sense of purpose and voicing it will ensure that all members of your team, including subcontractors and temporary employees, are on the same page. They, your employees will know precisely why your firm exists and who you serve.

Potential investors, lenders, and other strategic partners will also look to your stated purpose and corporate strategy to help assess whether your goals as a company align with theirs.

Your Mission Statement

Many Entrepreneurs I come across see having a mission

statement as a "feel good" thing to do. Most new business owners think of a mission statement as nothing more than a pie-in-the-sky statement that you write on your website to seem sophisticated. I happen to think this is the wrong way to look at your mission statement. Developing a well thought out mission statement based on your overall business goals is a crucial part of defining the purpose of your business.

So, What's a Mission Statement?

Well, I am glad you asked. In essence, a Mission Statement is a short, straight-to-the-point statement of purpose for your company. It is a summary of what you do as an organization. An effective Mission Statement will help you develop your long-term and short-term strategic objectives.

If you do your job correctly, all staff members, investors, and customers will be clear on what your company's mission statement is. You can easily create a killer mission statement by answering the question, "What business am I in?" An ideal Mission Statement should be one or two sentences long. Nothing lengthy or abstract. Now is not the time to get fancy. Avoid creating all-encompassing mission statements too. In other words, it makes no sense, for the purpose of communicating what you do to be verbose and/or try to be all things to all people.

Examples of Effective Mission Statements

Patagonia:
Build the best product, cause no unnecessary harm, use business to inspire and implement solutions to the environmental crisis.

JetBlue:
To inspire humanity – both in the air and on the ground.

Tesla:

To accelerate the world's transition to sustainable energy.

Universal Health Services, Inc.:
To provide superior quality healthcare services that:

PATIENTS recommend to family and friends,

PHYSICIANS prefer for their patients, PURCHASERS

select for their clients, EMPLOYEES are proud of, and

INVESTORS seek for long-term returns.

Honest Tea:
To create and promote great-tasting, healthy, organic beverages.

American Express:
We work hard every day to make American Express the

world's most respected service brand.

Your Vision Statement

Your Vision Statement will tell the story of where you want

to be upon the successful execution of your Mission

Statement. Your Vision Statement should also touch on how

you want to impact your community as a result of the existence of your business and how your products and services will ultimately benefit the world.

Within your Vision Statement, you will want to express any lofty aspirations you may have as a firm. Here you can feel free to be as expressive as you wish. Do not be afraid to throw in some feel-good statements and phrases, all while keeping your mission in mind.

Vision Statements from Well-Known Brands

Microsoft (at its founding):
A computer on every desk and in every home.

Creative Commons:
Realizing the full potential of the internet -- universal access to research and education, full participation in culture -- to drive a new era of development, growth, and productivity.

Alzheimer's Association:

A world without Alzheimer's disease.

What is your Value Proposition?

Your Customers' Success is your success.
A value proposition's definition is:

An innovation, service, or feature intended to make a company more attractive to customers.

The most important part of the value proposition is the customer; what about your product or service makes the customer want to buy from you? Is it price? Convenience? Branding?

What makes your business stand out from the field of competitors that compels the customer to buy from you? For example, you have three coffee shops on a block, one is a big brand, one is a Mom-and-Pop coffee shop, and one is a franchise-type coffee shop. Both of those shops are competing for customers. What is it that makes the customer choose one over the other?

Perhaps the big brand will attract customers because of brand messaging. The brand evokes a certain feeling. Customers having that cup of coffee in hand with a very recognizable logo makes them feel like they are part of an exclusive club because brand marketing has evoked those feelings in them. "We are saving the world, one cup of coffee at a time". Sound familiar?

What makes the Mom and Pop coffee shop stand out? Well, maybe they offer organic coffee, roast their coffee beans and provide a flavorful rich cup of coffee and advertise the best cup of coffee on the block, those that are particular about the quality of their coffee would be tempted to try them out.

Let's say the coffee shop served wine in the evening and

advertised in the surrounding neighborhood for folks to stop

by and have a glass of wine to unwind after work. A glass of

wine in the coffee shop in the evening will draw some

customers who might get to discover the great coffee they

offer and become a repeat customer.

My neighborhood grocery store recently installed a wine bar,

and surprisingly, business is booming! A grocery store bar

revealed that there was no place in the city that the 40-70

years old crowd can hang out. The value of the grocery store

bar to the customer is; I get to drink wine, and relax, in my

neighborhood, get to meet new people and take a load off.

We also have a franchise type store on the block. What

attracts customers to them? Well, coffee is an add-on item to

what they do best: fresh pastries! The customer goes to the

store for the pastries and, by suggestive selling, leaves the store with a coffee and a pastry and discovers that the coffee is delicious.

We have a French bakery in our city that is very popular. The authentic French Pastries took the city by storm and had customers waiting in long lines to sample their delicacies. Along with the pastry, they offer coffee and some light meals. Why do customers love them? They provide a unique, authentic experience and high-quality food that customers value.

So, when it comes to your business, ask yourself, what would the customer value? It is so important to home in on what would make your customers want your product.

Let's look at a service example; Two office cleaning firms go up for the same job, which is a small business with an office of 5 employees. What the small business owner is looking for is a company that does an excellent job at an affordable price.

The first cleaning company, call it company A, has worked with small businesses before and understands that price is essential to this size of business. Therefore, when submitting their proposal, they are quick to point out that they are the cheapest in town. Company B provides their proposal; they are licensed and bonded and use organic products; they can handle large and small clients but at a higher price. Company B will lose out on this contract because the customer, in this case, places the highest value on the price.

Say companies A and B go up for another job. This time it's a midsize company that owns their building. The business manager is worried about liability issues and wants someone who can handle the entire building. In this case, Company B will get the contract because they can point to their experience with large firms, they are licensed and bonded; therefore, if ever found liable for anything they would be covered. The fact that they use organic products would be a bonus!

So, the point is, when what your customer values, matches up with your offering, you have a transaction, do these many times over, and you have yourself a business.

How will you price your offering?

Coming up with an appropriate price for your products and services can be a tough nut to crack. Here, you face a dilemma as old as time itself. Set your prices too high, and you will surely have a difficult time attracting enough new customers to make a profit. Make your prices significantly lower than the rest of the market, and you will give the impression that your product or service is of lower quality than the rest in the marketplace. Plus, this strategy may not be sustainable long-term.

As a new business owner, setting the "right" price for your stuff is a task that you should not take lightly at all. Do not merely set prices based on your ego or view of what you think your firm's image is. Remember, your goal is profitability. Responding to the market's needs is a much easier way to get there.

I recommend you employ a three-dimensional view when considering what factors your prices are based upon: You should take a careful look at what your competitors charge as it relates to their level of service and service offerings. Do some research to see what their customers think of the pricing and try to figure out the income levels of consumers of your type of products.

Are these high net worth folks who buy these products as a symbol of wealth and luxury? Are these working folks who will take advantage of a deal of equal quality if they found one? Is your offering a "Must have" or "Would be nice to have"?

Also, consider the cost to produce your service or product. Any calculation of the cost of production should include salaries for yourself and your team, as well as marketing costs. Once you have completed your market analysis, it is time to figure out what your prices will be.

What would Walmart do?

If you decide to set your prices lower than that of your competitors to quickly attract customers, then you will want to build a marketing and overall business strategy that communicates your value to your customers. You will want to set clear expectations around your low prices and assure customers that quality is not lacking as a result of your more economical prices. You will want to tell a story that lets your customers know just how you can offer such low prices.

For Example:
"We own our factories, so we can cut out the middleman and pass the savings on to you."

We go to Walmart for the "Everyday Low prices" part of their messaging, and that's it. Nothing more, nothing less. The company communicates this value proposition clearly in all their messaging.

Think Outside the box

Pricing your products and services do not necessarily have to be a one-size-fits-all endeavor. Firms all over the world, these days have managed to formulate various exciting ways to price their offerings to suit the dynamic markets in which they operate. Global software companies like Microsoft will generally create varying pricing structures for similar products. Prices that conform to the market conditions in whichever country they are selling in.

On the other hand, Salesforce.com, the software giant created and spun-off Salesforce.org, a whole suite of their core products, but priced lower for their Non-profit customers. If affiliated with a school, online retail giant Amazon will offer extra discounts on their products. These are just a few examples of how companies can sell the same

products while employing a dynamic, creative approach to

pricing.

I urge you to dig deep and think of creative ways to price

your products and services in a way that offers value to your

customers, allows you to make a profit while setting you

apart from your competitors.

Examples of "Out-of-the-box" ways to approach pricing

Subscription model

Although some would argue that this type of approach to

pricing has been around for a long time, gym memberships,

cell phone services, and so forth. Where most agree is that

subscription-based pricing has become extremely popular

over the last ten years. Consumers are now, more than ever,

extremely comfortable with subscribing to an array of

products and services. The Average consumer these days has a bunch of services to which they subscribe. Netflix, Planet Fitness, Bulu Box, and many more.

According to a study conducted by research giant, McKinsey & Company, 15% of online shoppers have subscribed to an e-commerce service over the past year, with 46% of respondents subscribed to an online streaming-media service including Netflix. The most popular subscription services among consumers were Blue Apron, Dollar Shave Club, Ipsy and Stitch Fix. Subscription-based media includes Amazon Prime Video, Class Pass, Hulu, Netflix, Spotify, and others.

As a small business owner, you are in a unique position to capitalize on consumers' new-found love for subscription services. Especially, if your products or services fit into the "One-to-many" category. This category of products or services can be made available to multiple parties without the need to produce a new one. Software and personal, human-based services are excellent for this type of pricing model. Also, you want your product to be such that your customer will need to use it more than once and often.

Bundles
Pricing bundles or tiered offerings are great for products with many features. Inevitably, not all features will be deemed important by all users. So, what I am proposing here is to make a list of the services that you offer and plot out the features and map out what kinds of customers will want to use which features more than others.

Here, you will want to create various permutations of your customer profile (we will cover customer profiles later) and map out which features are benefits to which type of customer. With this in mind, create various bundles at different pricing levels to give your customers the ability to consume just what they need at a price they can afford.

Bundles also offer your customers a high starting point to get a chance to test out your products before upgrading to a package at a higher price point. Depending on your type of product, I would even ask that you consider offering a free bundle or basic bundle for a short time. The idea is to get new customers to try out your products.

Free plus
This approach to pricing will not fit with all kinds of products and services. It is one that is well suited for service offerings or products that require frequent maintenance. For example, if you build websites for your clients, you can offer basic web design for free and charge your customers an ongoing fee to maintain their websites. You can offer bundles of service at various pricing plans. For those who do

not require much upkeep, offer lower prices, and charge

higher rates for folks that need constant changes to their

websites.

Geo-based

Pricing your products and services based on the country in

which you are doing business works very well for small

business owners who are looking to offer products in

multiple countries. This approach will help you grow your

business while being sensitive to the economic situation of

the folks in those countries you operate.

You can partner with local firms and outreach groups to

offer discounts to their members, thus helping you ramp up

quickly and gaining instant credibility by working with a local

organization. Geo-based pricing is excellent for selling

products that can be accessed with an internet connection or are incredibly inexpensive to produce.

CHAPTER 1

HIGHLIGHTS

- When discussing your business, you should be able to explain to potential customers, potential investors or any interested party precisely what you do and how you would be able to add value to their lives and/or businesses. Try and refine your value statement to its simplest terms so that it is easily understood so that there is no ambiguity and fuzziness to what you do.

- Your mission statement essentially combines your goals and what you will do to get there in one concise sentence.

- Your vision statement declares what you hope to see after accomplishing your goals.

- Your Value Proposition is entirely customer focused on what will benefit the customer from purchasing your product/and or service. If you focus on the customer's needs and provide a solution for them at a price they can afford, then they are more likely to buy from you because you have presented value to them.

- You can implement a traditional pricing model based on the cost to produce the product or service and either offer it at a premium as a luxury good or offer it as a value price where customers can get a bargain.

- You can also employ a hybrid pricing strategy by offering a subscription fee pricing, or offer free initial services but charge for maintenance, or offer different bundles of products/services at various price points.

"People who succeed have momentum. The more they succeed, the more

they want to succeed, and the more they find a way to succeed. Similarly,

when someone is failing, the tendency is to get on a downward spiral that

can even become a self-fulfilling prophecy."

-Tony Robbins

CHAPTER 2

MARKET ANALYSIS

Get ready to do some spying

The market analysis portion of your business planning activities should consist of various activities that help you take a closer look at both qualitative and quantitative aspects of your market. A deep dive into all factors of your industry would be prudent. Lay out all possible elements, all there is to know about your space and determine how you can be the solution to any gaps or pain points the other guys have not addressed yet.

There are various platforms out there that can help you see what current and past customers think about your competitors and their products. Here, you will want to do some spying. Check out sites like Yelp, Glassdoor, Capterra, or any platform on which customers can provide feedback about their experiences with your competitors. Create a spreadsheet and catalog each type of complaint.

This simple activity will help you create an initial list of features and aspects of your business to magnify when trying to reach potential customers.

Small Fish in a Big Pond

Being "new" to your market, if approached correctly, can be of enormous economic and strategic advantage to you. Being 'The little guy", the Newbie, The Entrepreneur, can mean that you are nimbler than the rest of the guys and gals in the biz; giving you all the flexibility that comes with being small. You can move on new opportunities quicker than the rest of the competition. Sure, your industry certainly has well-established, well-funded players that may scare the bejesus out of you, and they should, but being a scrappy upstart also has some advantages.

Google, once a small, cash-strapped startup, at a time when companies like Yahoo and Ask Jeeves were making a killing serving up mediocre, often irrelevant search results, was able to capture market share by focusing on creating a platform that met the real needs of online searchers; Accurate search results.

By being small, the firm was able to respond to emerging market needs to become synonymous with an online search. Meanwhile, Yahoo was focused on becoming a media organization and ignored the opportunity to seize market share in the search space.

Feedback is your friend

Once you have:

1. Learned all that there is to know about your market

2. Have been able to work out how you intend to build your brand as the answer to the significant gaps in your industry that other companies fail to address

3. You have worked out how to communicate your value proposition to your prospective customers.

It's time to start thinking about how to reach out to some of the folks that might be interested in what you have to offer.

You will want to build a detailed customer profile which we will cover in detail in the next chapter and try to get them to buy or at the very least, try your product or service. The main goal here is to place yourself in a position to gather feedback from folks who have also tried your offering. Setup an automated system, via email or some other means, that will continually ask your new customers for feedback on how they think you can improve your offering. Do not let pride and ego get in the way of being the recipient of valuable input from the folks that matter the most; Your customers. Use the feedback you receive to help build new products and services and improve the existing ones.

Know your market

It is imperative to the success of your new business that you get to know your industry. You need to familiarize yourself with as much information about your market as possible. You will want to know the ins and outs of your business.

Industry Outlook

An in-depth look at any market as a whole or segment must begin with a complete analysis of the market, especially if you are new to this kind of business. Find out the overall size of your market, any innovations, the significant players in it, and any trends that may exist. Also, what is the projected growth of your overall market segment?

Demographics

The ideal target audience for your products and services will either be the general customer for your kind of business or a segment of the overall customer base. For example, the ideal target market for a midsize sedan may be the folks who are in Ford Motor Company's customer base. A $100,000 sports car, however, might be better suited and marketed to a segment of the general car-buying population. Here, many factors might differentiate the buyer of car one from two, but the main and apparent differences between both customers will be net worth, income, and gender, as expensive, "I am insecure about something" kind of cars are typically marketed to men.

Target Market

At this stage of the planning process, you want to assess and carefully lay out the target of your product or service. Here, you want to be very specific in creating a persona. Give this hypothetical customer a name. Learn everything there is to know about this type of person. Find out this person's gender, income levels, shopping habits, where they live, etc. This activity is what we call "building a customer profile."

If you are confused, don't worry, I will go into great detail about how to build in-depth customer profiles and the resources you need to do so in the next chapter. For now, keep in mind that knowing who your target market is, on a granular level, necessary for many reasons, especially for your marketing campaigns.

Total Addressable Market
The Total Addressable Market (T.A.M.) is the growth potential your business has concerning the total number of

potential customers. In other words, how many people will benefit from your offering? You must ask yourself, "Is my business going to address a significant problem in a big enough market?"

Assessing (with the help of market research) how many folks in your market can benefit, or whose lives will become easier or improved, as a result of your product, will help you build marketing, and overall business strategy to reach out to your core audience.

Rules and Regulations
What are the State and Federal regulations required to enter and operate in your market? Map out a plan to adhere to these rules and regulations and how to stay compliant as your business grows and evolves.

Market Need

Market need is about figuring out or trying to figure out the main reasons why your prospective customers will need or want your product or service. What precisely will motivate your prospects to spend their hard-earned money on what you are selling. At this stage, you want to take a closer look at the behavior of folks in your target market to prove to yourself or any partners or potential investors why you think people will do business with your company.

One effective but inexpensive way to gauge market need is by observing the behavior of your competitors' current customers. By doing so, you can often discover and capitalize on needs in the market left unmet by your most significant competitors.

Competition

One of the most critical parts of any detailed market research is to determine who the other players in the game are. Whom

will you be going up against once you jump into any given

market? It is essential for you to do some systematic spying

on the competition. You will be surprised at how much you

can learn about the business you are in, or going into, by

doing some basic research on your competitors.

My approach is creating a spreadsheet with details about your

top ten biggest competitors and making detailed notes about

what their customers say about them which is easy to do

these days since we all freely share our opinions online about

everything online. Try to determine the strengths and

weaknesses of your competitors as told by their customers.

Pro tip:
You can build your startup to specifically address a complaint

the market has about your most significant competitor and

be sure to mention that in your marketing.

For example, if your competitor's customers complain that a news article found their product is not 100% organic, you can make it a point to source pure organic produce and build your messaging around that differentiator. "At X.Y.Z. company, when we say Organic, we mean 100% organic".

COMPETITIVE ANALYSIS LANDSCAPE

Complete the template for your company, then complete the template for each competitor. After you complete this form, you may find out that your competitors are not who you think they are.

		YOUR COMPANY	COMPETITOR 1	COMPETITOR 2	COMPETITOR 3
	WHY CONDUCT THIS ANALYSIS?	Write down the question you are trying to answer or the goal of this analysis			
PROFILE	OVERVIEW				
	COMPETITIVE ADVANTAGE What value do you offer customers?				
MARKETING PROFILE	TARGET MARKET				
	MARKETING STRATEGIES				
PRODUCT PROFILE	PRODUCTS & SERVICES				
	PRICING & COSTS				
	DISTRIBUTION CHANNELS				
SWOT ANALYSIS	STRENGTHS	Do this for your company and for your competitors. Your strengths should support your opportunities and contribute to what you define as your competitive advantage.			
	WEAKNESSES				
	OPPORTUNITIES				
	THREATS				

Competitive Analysis Template. Source: www.smartsheet.com

CHAPTER 2

HIGHLIGHTS

- The market analysis looks at the size of the market both in volume and value, various customer segments, buying patterns, competition, and barriers to entry in terms of regulations and economics.

- You can start your market analysis by looking at websites where customers can provide public feedback on their service/product. You should make a note of the complaints and address them specifically in your offering to differentiate yourself from the crowd.

- Being a new business can be an advantage as you are small and flexible enough to act on new trends.

- Familiarize yourself with every aspect of your industry, the size, the primary market shareholders, any regulation changes, or any upcoming trends.

- Demographics studies determine your most likely customers based on characteristics such as age, income, gender, geographical location. You can use this information to build a customer profile, by studying the desired demographics lifestyle and shopping habits.

"Success seems to be connected with action. Successful people keep moving. They make mistakes, but they don't quit."

-Conrad Hilton

CHAPTER 3

CUSTOMER PROFILE

Launching a business which stands a chance at any measure of success involves multiple "Must get just right" steps. My recommendation to new business owners or anyone thinking about starting a business is to take the time to conduct ample research and planning.

As old school as it may sound to some, we strongly suggest that anyone looking to launch a new venture take the time out to create three plans; A business and marketing plan as well as a capital or funding strategy and a comprehensive customer profile.

In this chapter, we shall take a closer look at what a customer profile is, the importance of creating an in-depth customer profile, and take a look at customer profiles from some top brands. By the time you are through with this book, hopefully, we would have been able to add some value and provided some insights to help you start your new business or grow your current startup.

What is a customer profile?

The first step to creating an effective customer profile, as far as this book is concerned, is to get a general understanding of what a customer profile is. A customer profile or customer persona is a detailed description of your ideal customer. You will have an easier time creating a customer profile if you already have some paying customers at this point in your business.

You will have to compile a list of common demographic and

geographic traits shared among most of your customers. For example, once you start to create a table to plot your customer attributes, you may notice that most of your customers are women of a certain age, with similar ethnic backgrounds, professions, and marital status.

New businesses will have to conduct some basic research to create a customer cutout, a placeholder of sorts, a temporary customer persona based on the kind of customers who typically buy products like yours. You can use the tools provided by Esri to develop a preliminary customer profile.

In some circles, a complete customer profile will take the form, theoretically, of an avatar. Your avatar should be fully developed, with a name, ethnicity, age, and other physical attributes. Focus on the characteristics that make your typical customer a prime candidate for spending their money with you.

Being aware of these traits will help you adopt a dynamic marketing strategy. One that speaks to your customer in every aspect of their lives. In this chapter, we will look at some compelling customer profiles from top global brands.

Importance of Customer Profiles

Your goal as a small business owner is ultimately to sell as many products or find as many clients for your service(s) as humanly possible. You should continually be engaged in the pursuit of selling more while streamlining your overall cost structure. By that I mean, you should always be on the lookout for opportunities to reduce your costs, while selling more.

If you are a solopreneur, like most small business owners are, then I assure you that your most considerable business expense is or is going to be your sales and marketing costs. It is going to be a freaking balancing act trying to reduce your marketing costs to allow maximum profitability.

At the beginning of your venture, that goal is going to seem almost impossible to achieve, but trust me, with some careful planning and strategic marketing, you will find a way to squeeze out a respectable profit margin. As time goes on, and your firm grows beyond your first 100 customers, you will want to, as much as possible, reduce your cost per customer acquisition. That is to say, the dollar amount it costs to get each paying customer. This amount may vary at times based on overall marketing costs, seasonality, the proliferation of a product or service, competition, and customer attrition.

One of the most effective ways to drive down your overall

marketing costs and save time is to target only the individuals or firms which most likely need/want your products and services.

Marketing a product or service meant for companies with over 100 employees to small businesses with average teams of up to four members will be a waste of time and money since your product would not be appropriate for them even if they were interested. Most Entrepreneurs make the mistake of trying to sell their stuff to anyone and everyone. Resist the temptation to do so. Focus on a targeted group of potential customers for maximum return on investment.

Here, Customer profiling is your best friend. Building a complete customer profile, or persona(s) of prospective customers will help reduce your marketing costs.

Creating a customer profile will allow you to:

- Create additional complementary products and services to offer to your existing customer base. You will make more money per customer, and you won't have to spend much money to acquire these customers as they will already be in your contacts database.

- Provide world-class customer service since you will be familiar with the unique needs and wants of your ideal customer. You may, for example, see it prudent to extend your customer service hours to accommodate your customers once you find out that a significant portion of them work third shift or are overseas. We chose to do so at our Software company, once we found out that 20% of our customers were outside the United States.

- Create promotions and discounts specifically for their lifestyles and needs.

How to build a customer profile

Building a customer profile for your new or existing business venture can be a straightforward task or complex undertaking depending on the nature of your business and the diversity among your offerings. Believe it or not, individual, non-business consumers make for the most complex personas.

The genesis of your customer profile creation process should be to first gather as much information about your ideal customer as possible. What is your ideal customers' age range, occupation, hobbies, income, marital status, and so forth? Use this information, gathered by analyzing your existing customer data or research, to build a comprehensive customer profile.

Qdoba, the popular Mexican fast-food chain, calls its ideal

customer "Quintessa." The company based their avatar on various movie characters including Jennifer Lawrence's character in "Silver Lining" and Uma Thurman's character in "Pulp Fiction" and "Kill Bill."

Customer Profile: Quentessa (Qdoba)

Age: 32

Occupation: Professional

Marital Status: Single

Income: $100,000 per year

Hobbies: Loves going out with friends and enjoys a good movie, occasionally.

Elements of a Customer Profile

Before you start building your ideal customer profile, you must know what types of data is needed and which kinds of information you can omit. While there are many different opinions out there about what information to include in a customer profile, most experts agree that an ideal customer profile should, at the very least include demographic, socioeconomic, and psychographic data.

Your customer profile should include the following:

Demographic:

Age- The age range of your ideal customer. Typically, a 10-20-year age range is recommended.

Gender- What are the percentages of males versus females among your customer base. The higher would be the stencil upon which to base your ideal customer profile, as far as gender is concerned.

Ethnicity/Race- What race or ethnicity constitutes the most significant percentage of your customer base or likely customers?

Socioeconomic:

Average Household Income – What is the average household income of your ideal customer. Here, you want to get an estimate of how much your typical customer or ideal prospective customer makes per year.

Level of education- What level of education, on average, does your ideal customer have?

Occupation – What type of work does your average customer do for a living. Feel free to get as specific or as general as you wish based on how relevant this information is to your marketing needs.

Community/Neighborhood- In what type of environment does your ideal customer live? Are the bulk of your customers inner-city dwellers or suburbanites?

Household Description-What is the family makeup of your average customer's household? Are they single, single with kids, married, or living with a partner?

Psychographics:

Hobbies – What do your ideal customers do for fun or enjoy doing in their spare time? Are they volunteers and/or donors, or do they like to take vacations to get away from the monotony of their daily lives?

Interests – What are your customer's interests? What gets them excited?

Favorite Entertainment Choices – Where do they go for news? What radio stations

Anxieties – What makes your ideal customers, and most of your current customers, fearful? Do they have any worries your business can help alleviate?

Examples of customer profiles

Pamela Power Shopper

Demographics:

Age: 32 years
Gender: female
Marital Status: Married
(2 young kids)
Location: Austin

Occupation:

Housewife

Annual Income:

$0 (high earning husband)

Education:

College

Behavior:

Pamela...
• Buys heavily online
• Expert level shopper
• Great spending power
• Buys for her family daily needs as well
• Frequently buys gifts for friends and family

Goals:

Pamela wants...
• Frequent product inspirations
• Great recommendations
• New, popular and trending things
• Event based reminders about products

Objections to the sale:

• Not her taste

Channel:

• Mostly online, in-store purchases
are very rare

Pain Points:

Pamela's pain points are...
• No inspirations for buying and trying out
new things
• High delivery charges and taxes

Motivations:

Pamela is motivated by...
• High personalization
• Quick shopping features and fast transactions
• Good gifting product suggestions
• Great savings on product bundles

Devices:

• Mobile, tablet and laptop but mostly mobile

Key Strategies:

• Create a loyalty program for such frequent buyers.
• Analyze her purchase history and other data
points to recommend products for her next
purchase.
• Encourage her to try out new products showing
high value in new products.

Example of a Customer Profile

Ann

Who they are:
- 61
- Widow, (Grand) Mother.
- Income: $ 72,320
- 25 year fulltime teacher High School, History
- Bachelor degree History, UCLA.
- Suburban area in SoCal, USA
- Has a lot of beader friends; virtual as well as IRL.
- Bling is her 6 year old Yorkshire Terrier.

What they think:
- 20+ year beader who prefers mixed media projects.
- Online reading Beading Daily, bead blogs, bead instructor Facebook pages.
- Subscribes to beading magazines.
- Wants to learn new techniques.
- Fan of: Kleo Pham Gray, Kim St. Jean, and Lorelei Eurto.

What they do:
- Spends $ 200 per month on beading supplies.
- Buys at webshops and at Etsy.
- Attends Bead & Button every year, to meet with friends.
- Takes online beading classes at Beaducation.
- Is a member of the San Diego Beading Society.
- She sells her jewelry on Etsy and some local/church events.

Where they operate:
- Shops mainly in USA although is venturing internationally through Etsy.

Ann's life revolves around teaching, learning, beading, her dog, and grandkids. She converted one of the spare bedrooms into a beading studio where she spends most of her evenings making jewelry. She has an enormous online circle of beader friends. When she retires she plans to bead full time and will start to teach beading locally and maybe even write a beading book.

DOTS N INK
MARKETING & MEDIA

TOBI DAY

PERSONA TEMPLATE

AGE 26
OCCUPATION Record Store Manager
STATUS Single
LOCATION New York, NY

TIER Enthusiast
ARCHETYPE The Maestro

Ambitious   Admired   Focused

"If I had a way to share projects and collaborate in real time, that would make my workload so much easier to manage."

MOTIVATIONS

GOALS

- To grow a strong industry reputation
- To build an audio-pro portfolio
- To keep track of everything

FRUSTRATIONS

- Slow download times
- Data crashes
- Poor communication

BIO

Tobi has a day job at a record store, but on the side she does all kinds of production work for up-and-coming artists. She never hesitates to learn something new and she often acts as tech support for her friends and clients. She is usually working on a dozen projects at a time and is trying to establish herself in the industry, so she hates data crashes or anything that makes her look bad. Because she works alone and in her home, collaboration is everything.

PERSONALITY

Extrovert   Introvert

Sensing   Intuition

Thinking   Feeling

Judging   Perceiving

TECHNOLOGY

IT and Internet

Software

Mobile Apps

Social Networks

75

CHAPTER 3

HIGHLIGHTS

- A customer profile is a detailed description of your ideal customer.

- Creating a customer profile lowers your marketing costs because you can target those that are most likely to buy with advertising. It will also help you create complementary products that your ideal customers could use.

- Your customer profile should include demographic data like age and gender as well as psychographic data like hobbies, anxieties, and entertainment.

RESOURCES

Business Planning

SBA.gov

Market Research

- For general business US. census. Bureau,

- Industry research-USA.gov statistics

- Competition research- Glassdoor.com, Yelp.com

- Demographics - Bureau of Labor and Statistics

- Market Segmentation and Customer profile- Esri.com

- Consumer Behavior/ spending- bea.gov

ABOUT THE AUTHOR

FRANK

I started my first business at the age of 16. It was a tiny

online retailer of consumer electronics. We sold stuff like

DVD Players, Digital Cameras, and Cordless phones before

online shopping was a thing everyone did. Before Facebook

and Instagram.

The venture failed. My first company crashed and burned for

many reasons, the least of which was poor planning and the

lack of a cohesive strategy. I would love to say I learned a lot

from my first failure, but the truth is, by the time it all went

down in flames, I was just over it and ready to move on.

I would not venture into the world of business again until

twelve years later. I started a small insurance firm with the woman who would become my wife. Our company got off

to a rocky start, and we had to endure many setbacks.

Today, our tiny Insurance Agency has morphed into several

companies. We now have our hands in all kinds of business,

including software and real estate.

ABOUT THE AUTHOR

GATHONI

Miss. Gathoni Njenga is an entrepreneur and author. She currently serves as the Co-Founder of Corvus Web Services, a software development firm. She is also the General Agent and founder of UES Benefits, a full-service insurance services company. She is also a board member and investor in several Real Estate companies in Kenya. Gathoni Njenga is currently based in the U.S.A, where she runs her businesses and loves to write in her spare time.

www.ingramcontent.com/pod-product-compliance
Lightning Source LLC
Chambersburg PA
CBHW030727180526
45157CB00008BA/3070